WORKBOOK

New Parade

Starter

Senior Authors

Mario Herrera

Theresa Zanatta

Consulting Authors

Alma Flor Ada   Anna Uhl Chamot   Jim Cummins

Christine Ewy   Carolyn Kessler   J. Michael O'Malley

Writer

Mary E. Reid

Longman

Acknowledgments

Consulting Reviewers

Brigite Fonseca, Colegio Bom Jesus de Joinville, Joinville, Brazil • **Cleide da Silva**, Openhouse Ensino de Inglés, Santos, Brazil • **Luz Marina Franco**, Colegio El Carmelo, Santafé de Bogotá, Colombia • **Irene Gómez de Reina and Mariela Quintero**, Liceo Patria, Santafé de Bogotá, Colombia • **Magdalena Moreno**, Liceo Naval, Santafé de Bogotá, Colombia • **Maribel Muñoz**, Escuela Holanda, Ministerio de Educación Pública, San Jose, Costa Rica • **Cynthia de Cano**, Instituto Guatemalteco Americano, Guatemala City, Guatemala • **Keiko Abé-Ford**, Communication and Language Associates, Tokyo, Japan • **Francis Acosta López Serdán, Vanessa Olvera Vega, and Maria del Pilar Paez Laguna**, Colegio Guadalupe, Mexico City, Mexico • **Maricela Camino**, Centro Escolar Yaocalli, Mexico City, Mexico • **Jean Pierre Brossard**, Proulex, Guadalajara, Mexico • **Maggie Fabrian del Conde**, Instituto Felix de Jesus Rougier, Mexico City, Mexico • **Elsa Jiménez**, SEPC Primary English Program, Saltillo, Mexico • **Ruth Jossa Valtierra and Myriam Romero Muñoz**, Colegio Tepeyac, Mexico City, Mexico • **Raquel Loaiza**, Escuela Loaiza de Inglés, Reynosa, Mexico • **Mary Margaret Rose**, Sultanate Private School, Madinal Qaboos, Oman • **Angie Alcocer**, Colegio Maria Alvarada, Lima, Peru • **Walter Alvarez**, Colegio Santa Teresita, Lima, Peru • **Silvia Osores**, Colegio Immaculada, Lima, Peru • **Anna Marie Amudi**, Dhahran Ahliyya School, Dammam, Saudi Arabia • **Denise Özdeniz**, Teacher Trainer, Istanbul, Turkey • **Youssef Arifi**, Al Ghazali School, Abu Dhabi, United Arab Emirates • **Lupita Arraga**, Colegio Bellas Artes, Maracaibo, Venezuela • **María Gabriela de Pressutto**, Colegio IDEA, Valencia, Venezuela • **María Elena Izaguirre**, Colegio Canigua, Caracas, Venezuela • **Silvia Landa**, Secretaría de Educación, Carabobo, Venezuela • **Carmen Mendoza**, Colegio Emil Friedman, Caracas, Venezuela

New Parade Starter Workbook

Editorial director: Louise Jennewine
Publisher: Anne Stribling
Director of design and production: Rhea Banker
Development editor: Mary Ann Ryan
Production manager: Alana Zdinak
Managing editor: Linda Moser
Senior production editor: Mike Kemper
Manufacturing supervisor: Dave Dickey
Cover design: Pearson Education Development Group
Art direction and production: Pearson Education Development Group

Illustrations Page abbreviations are as follows: (T) top, (B) bottom, (L) left, (R) right, (C) center.

Ellen Appleby 61, 62, 63, 65, 66, 67; Paige Billin-Fry 52, 53, 54, 55, 58, 59, 60; Nan Brooks 17, 20, 22; Daniel Del Valle 82, 84, 85(B), 86, 88; Mena Dolobowsky 7, 9, 10, 11, 12, 13, 15, 16, 23, 27, 30, 40, 43, 78, 83, 85(T), 87(T), 91; Patrick Girouard 1, 2, 3, 4, 5, 8; Tim Haggerty 61, 72, 73, 89; Susan T. Hall 29, 31, 32, 33, 34, 44, 57; Ben Mahan 22, 87(B); John Nez 52, 53; Laura Ovresat 24, 25, 26, 45, 47, 50, 51, 81, 83(T); Chris Powers 17, 42; Chris Reed 41, 48, 49, 77; Doug Roy 35, 37, 38, 39, 42, 68, 74; Stan Tusan 69, 71, 72, 73, 75, 76.

Picture Dictionary Art Patti Green 1–8; David Sheldon 9–16; Myron Grossman 19–24; Janice Skivington 29–34; Slug Signorino 37–42; Shirley Beckes 43–50; Linda Kelen 53–60; Donna Reynolds 61–68; Laurie Hamilton 69–76.

Cover and Title Page Art Tracy M. Lee

Pearson Education, 10 Bank Street, White Plains, NY 10606

ISBN: 0-201-62980-1

7 8 9 10 — BAH — 05 04 03

Contents

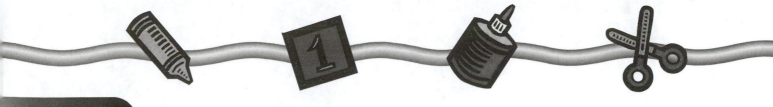

1 My Class

1. Trace and color.

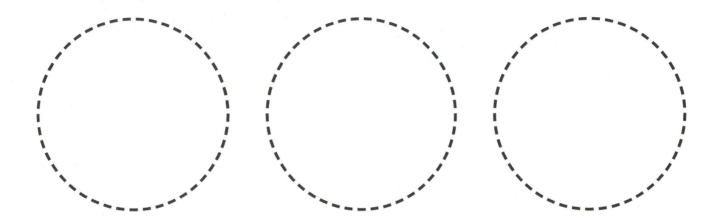

2. Color the circles.

Students trace, count, and color circles. They color one circle
red and two circles yellow. They find and color circles in a scene.

3. Count and match.

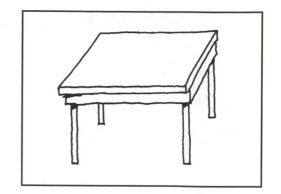

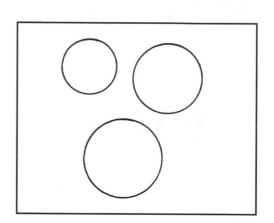

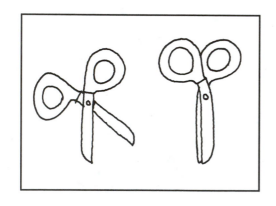

Students count and match sets of objects.

4. Match. Draw a line.

Students draw lines from the items in the picture
to the matching items at the bottom of the page.

5. Listen and color.

Students listen to the directions and color items red or yellow.

6. Cut. Put. Say.

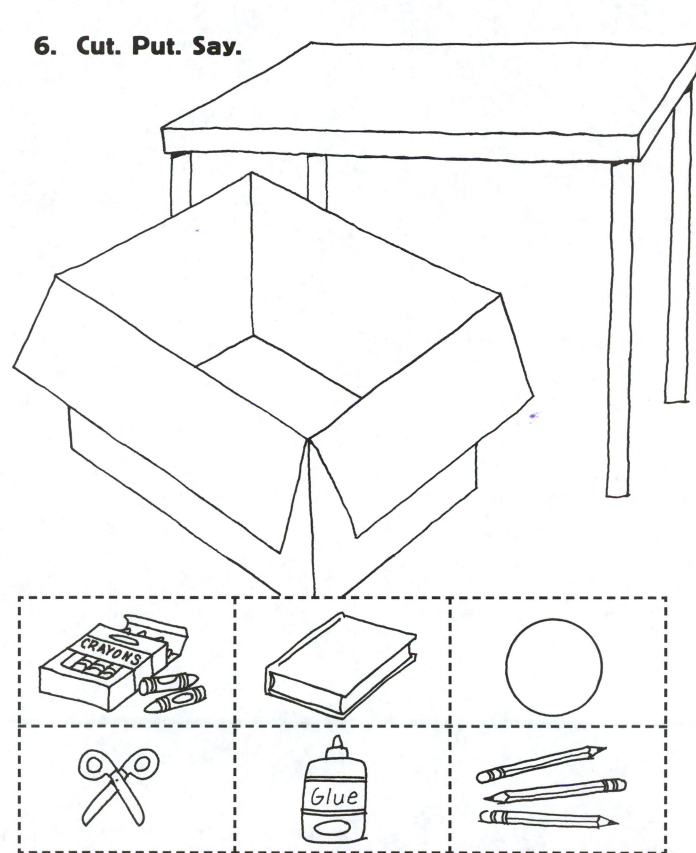

Students cut and put items **in** a box or **on** a table.
They say **in** or **on** to tell where they have put each one.

7. Color the spaces.

1 = red 2 = yellow

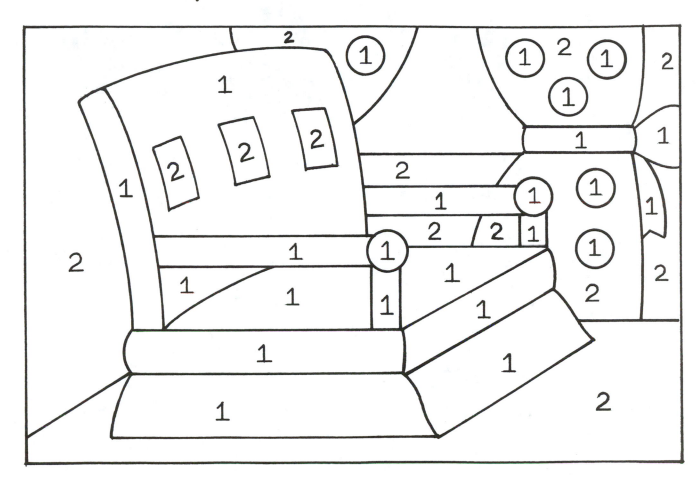

8. What is it? Circle.

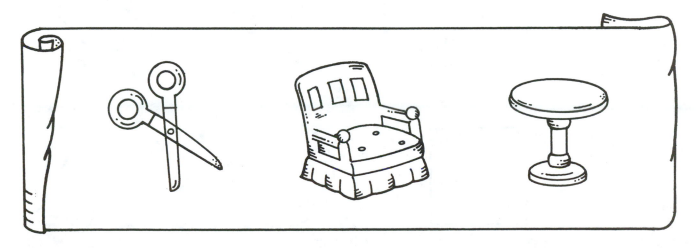

Students color spaces according to a color code
to make a red chair on a yellow background.

UNIT 1 • My Class   7

✔ Listen. Circle. 🎧

1.

2.

3.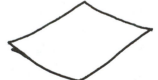

4.

5.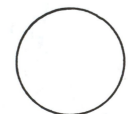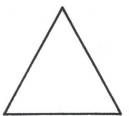

2 My Home

1. Find. Match. Draw lines.

Students draw lines from the people in the picture
to the matching people at the bottom of the page.

2. Count. Circle.

1. **2   3   4**

2. **2   3   4**

3. **2   3   4**

4. **2   3   4**

5. **2   3   4**

6. **2   3   4**

3. Trace. Write.

Students count and circle the number of people in
each picture. They trace and write numerals 1–4.

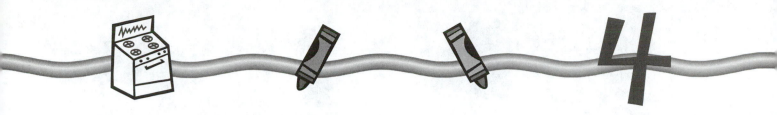

4. Count. Match. Draw lines.

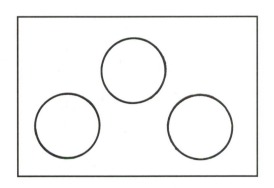

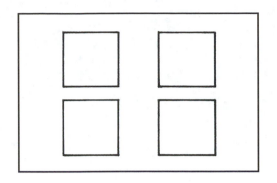

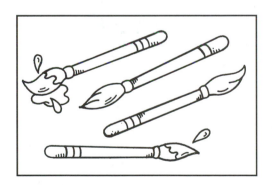

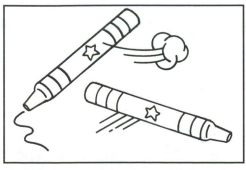

Students count and match sets that have the same number of objects.

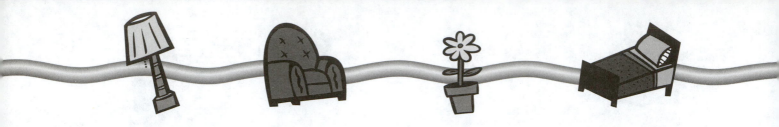

5. Trace.

6. Color. Draw.

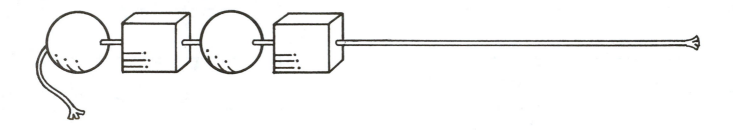

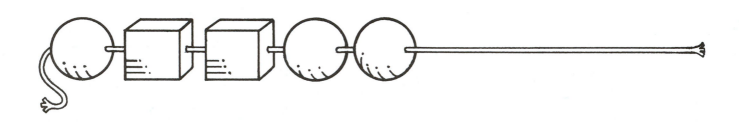

Students trace a circle and a square. They color the circles blue and the squares green, and draw more circles and squares.

7. Cut. Listen. Glue.

Students cut out items. They listen and place
the items **in** a room or **on** a table.

8. Draw.

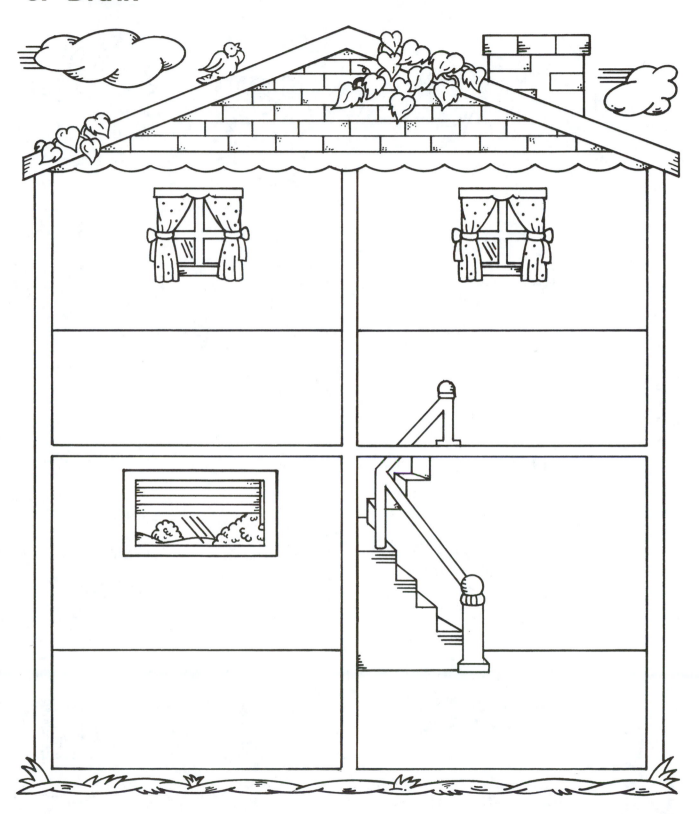

Students draw family members in the house.
They draw furniture in appropriate rooms.

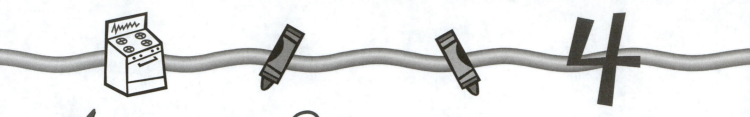

Listen. Circle.

1.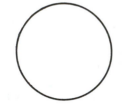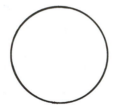

2.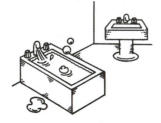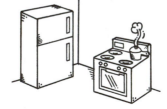

3.

4.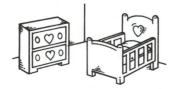

5.

3 My Body

1. Color. Cut. Play a game.

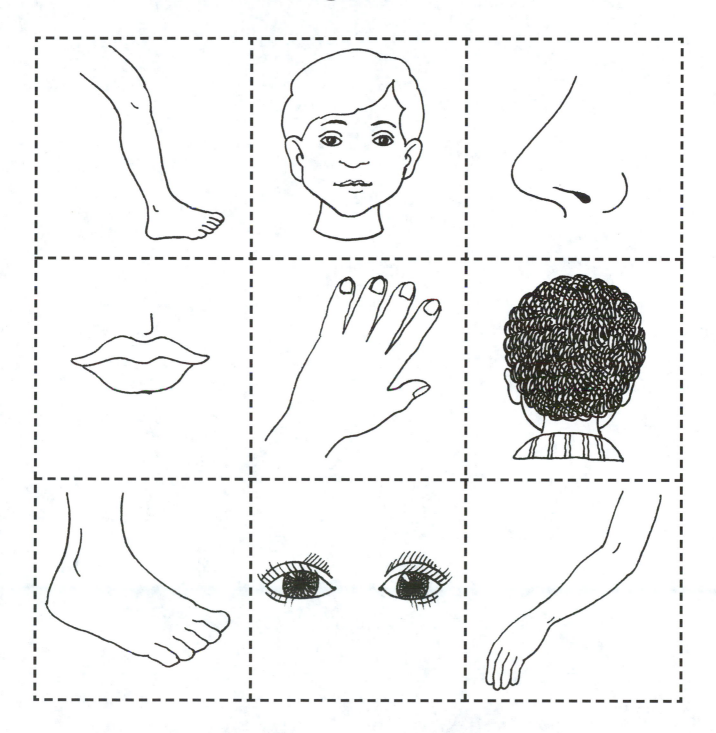

Students cut out cards that represent body parts. They
play memory and matching games with the cards.

2. Count. Color.

3 ◯ ◯ ◯ ◯ ◯ ◯

4 ▢ ▢ ▢ ▢ ▢ ▢

5 △ △ △ △ △ △

3. Trace. Write.

4. Draw. Color.

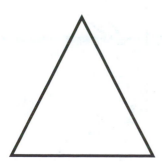

Students review numerals **3–5** by coloring that number of shapes in each row. They trace and write numerals **2–5**. They draw and color **5** triangles.

5. Count. Write.

 _____

 _____

 _____

 _____

Students identify and count body parts and write numerals.

6. Look. Color.

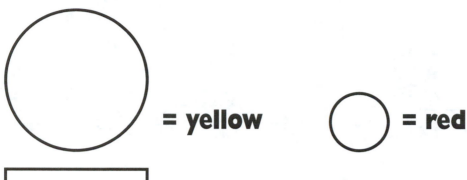

= yellow   ◯ = red

= green   ▢ = blue

= brown   △ = black

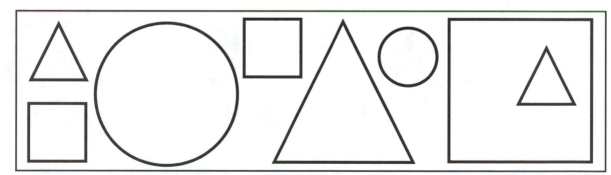

7. Trace. Color. Draw.

Students use a color code to color shapes. They trace a square and color it blue.
They trace a triangle and color it orange. They draw more squares and triangles.

8. Listen. Circle.

1.

2.

3.

4.

5.

Students listen and circle pictures that illustrate the prepositions
in, **on**, and **under**, and the feelings **sad** and **happy**.

9. Draw. Color.

Students draw themselves and a friend
having fun on a playground.

1.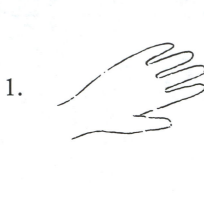

2.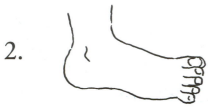

3.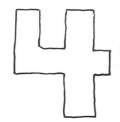

4.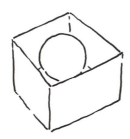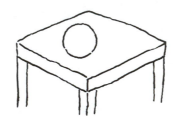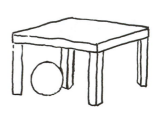

5.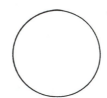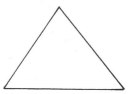

Units 1-3 Test

Listen. Circle.

1.

2.

3.

4.

5.

6.

Listen. Circle.

1.

2.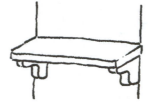

3.

4.

5.

6.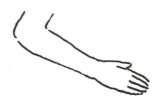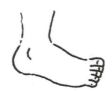

4 My Clothes

1. Color. Cut. Play a game.

Students color and cut out clothing cards. They make an outfit together.
Then they play a memory or matching game with a partner.

2. Listen. Color. 🎧

3. Count. Write. How many?

_____4_____

Students listen and color items as directed.
They count pictured items and write numerals.

UNIT 4 • My Clothes   29

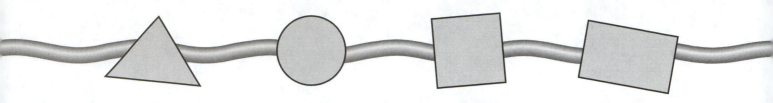

4. Color. Drop. Say.

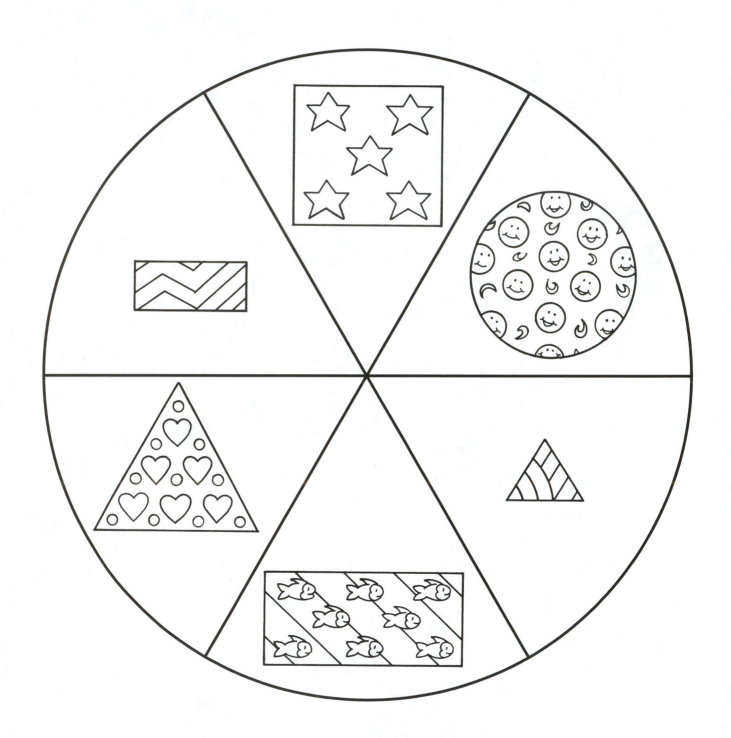

Students color shapes and then drop a marker on the circular game board. They name the shape, size, and color of the object that the marker falls on.

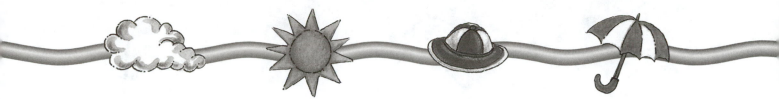

5. Color. Match.

Students match clothing to appropriate weather.

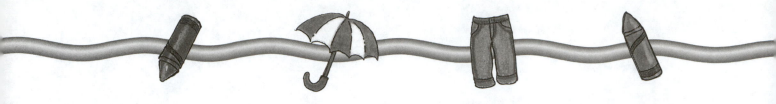

6. Draw yourself in the right kind of clothing.

Students draw themselves in clothes appropriate for a rainy day and for a sunny day.

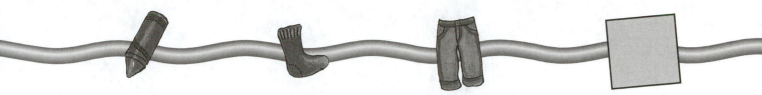

7. Listen. Color. Play Bingo.

Students listen and color. Then they listen and play Bingo, finding each item as it is named. They say, "Bingo!" if they cover three in a row.

 Listen. Circle.

1.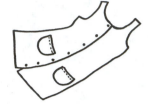

2.

3.

4.

5.

6.

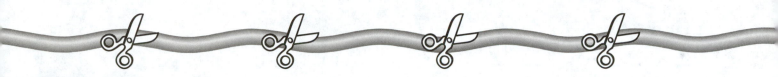

5 My Toys

1. Color. Cut. Play a game.

Students color and cut out cards. They play
memory or matching games with the cards.

UNIT 5 • My Toys   35

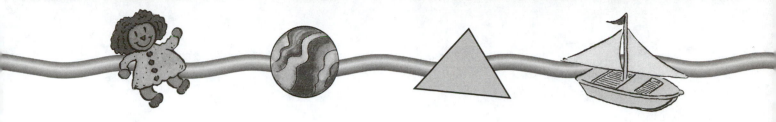

2. Count. Color.

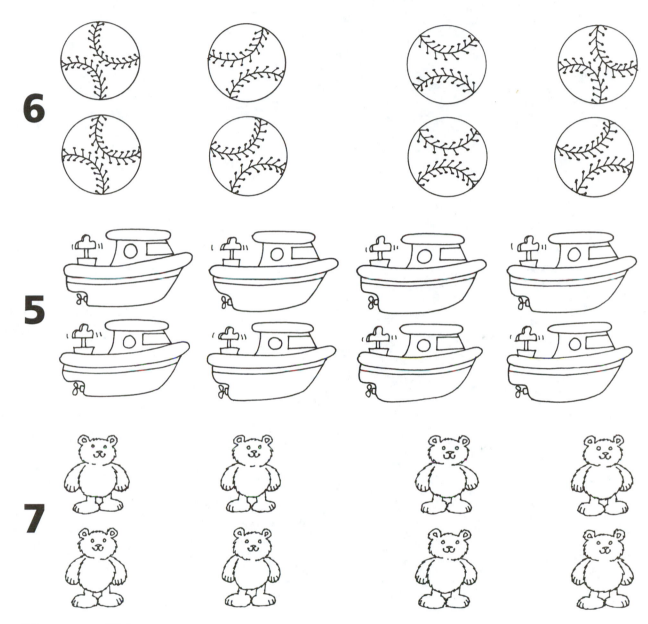

6

5

7

3. Trace. Write.

Students color the number of toys indicated by a numeral.
They trace and write the numerals **6** and **7**.

4. Draw and color four toys.

Students draw four toys and color one green, one orange, one pink, and one blue.

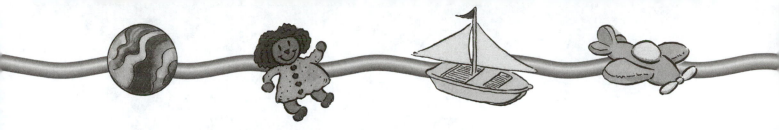

5. Write the number. How many?

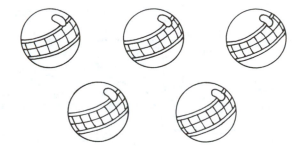

_____

_____

_____

Students count toys and write the correct number.

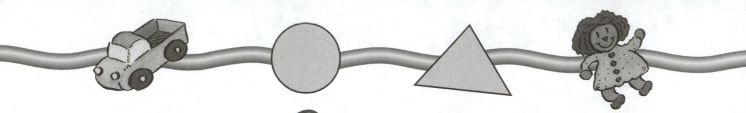

6. Listen. Color.

7. Count. Write.

Students identify shapes and color them as directed.
They count the shapes and write the number of each.

8. Play a game!

Start

Go Back 2 Spaces

Go Back 2 Spaces

End!

Students play a game, naming the toy or number of shapes on each space they land on.

UNIT 5 • My Toys   41

Listen. Circle.

1.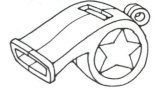

2.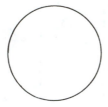

3.

4.

5.

   5   **6**   **7**

6.

   5   **6**   **7**

6 Helpers

1. Color the shapes.

Circles = purple. Squares = blue. Triangles = green.
Rectangles = yellow.

2. Count. Write.

△ _____   ◻ _____   ○ _____   ▢ _____

Students find shapes and color each kind of shape by following
the color code. They count the shapes and write the numerals.

UNIT 6 • Helpers   43

3. Color. Count.

8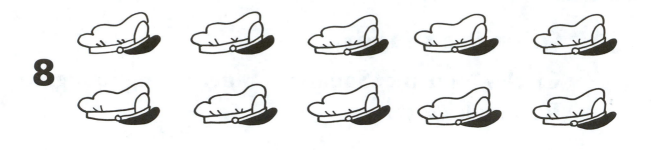

9

7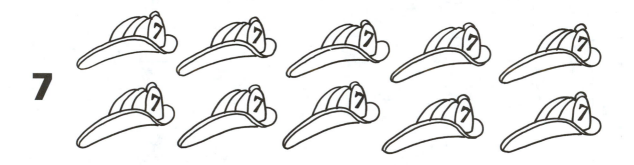

4. Trace. Write

Students count items and color the number indicated by a numeral. They trace and write the numerals 8 and 9.

5. Cut. Glue.

Glue the helpers where they help.

1.

2.

3.

Students cut out and glue helpers to complete scenes where they are needed.

6. Listen. Circle.

1.

2.

3.

4.

5.

Students listen to a sentence and circle
the picture that shows the action.

7. Match. Draw a line.

1.

2.

3.

4.

5.

6.

Students draw lines to connect helpers with their tools and vehicles.

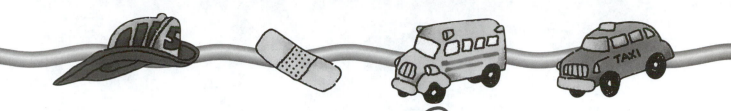

8. Listen. Color. Play Bingo.

Students listen and color. Then they listen and play Bingo, finding each item as it is named. They say, "Bingo!" if they cover three in a row.

Listen. Circle.

1.

2.

3.

4.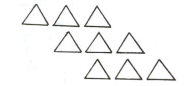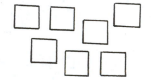

5.

6.

✔ Units 4–6 Test

Listen. Circle.

1.

2.

3.

4.

5.

6.

✔ Listen. Circle. 🎧

1. 　　　

2. 　　　

3. 　　　

4. ☐　　　▭

5. ◯　　　◦

6. ☐　　　☐

✔ Say how many things you circled.

7 The Playground

1. Listen. Circle.

Students listen and circle with different colored crayons to identify the child doing each action.

2. Count. Match. Draw a line.

3. Trace. Draw 10 balls.

Students count objects and match groups that have the same number of objects. They draw **10** balls.

4. Cut. Glue.

Students cut and glue figures of children in the appropriate places on the playground.

5. Listen. Find. Color.

Students listen to directions and color children who are **in**, **out**, **on**, or **under** something, or are going **up**, **down**, or **off**.

6. Connect the dots from 1 to 10.

Draw a friend.

Students count to **10** as they follow the dots to draw a slide under the boy. They draw a friend for him.

7. Draw. Color. Tell.

Students draw themselves and a friend playing at a playground.
They say where they are and what they are doing.

 Listen. Circle.

1.

2.

3.

4.

5.

6.

8 Animals

1. Match. Circle.

Name the animal. Circle the one that matches.

1.

2.

3.

4.

5.

6.

Students name an animal and circle an identical animal in the same row.

UNIT 8 • Animals 61

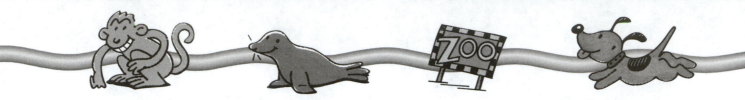

2. Listen. Circle.

1.

2.

3.

4.

5.

6.

Students listen and circle the animal or person described.

3. Cut. Glue.

Pets

Zoo Animals

Students cut out zoo animals and pets and place them in the appropriate circles.

4. Help the baby find its mother.

Draw a path.

Students find paths through the maze so that each baby zoo animal can find its mother.

5. Draw. Color.

Students draw four animals—one **eating**, one **resting**, one **playing**, and one **walking**.

6. Draw. Follow the numbers.

7. Count. Color.

8

9

10

Students follow numbers to draw a bear. They
count and color **8**, **9**, and **10** animals.

Listen. Circle.

1.

2.

3.

4.

5.

6.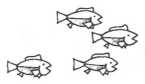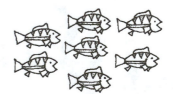

9 Party Food

1. Cut. Glue.

1.

2.

3.

4.

Students cut out pictures of foods, match them with foods shown on the page, and glue them in place to complete pictures.

2. Draw. Color.

Students draw and color a cake, two plates, two cups, and two forks.

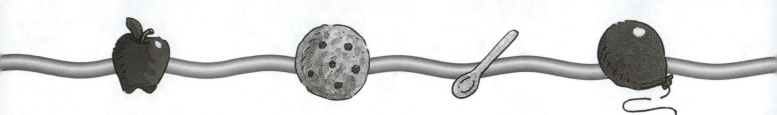

3. Count. Match.

Draw a line.

5

6

7

8

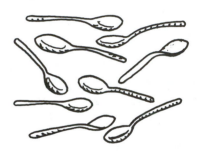

9

10

4. Count. Write.

Write the missing numbers.

1 ___ **3** ___ ___ **5 6** ___ **8** ___ ___

Students count objects in a group and draw a line to the correct numeral. They fill in numbers in a sequence.

5. Listen. Circle.

1.    

2.    

3.    

4.    

5.    

Students listen and circle the person
doing each action named.

6. Circle the one that is different.

1.

2.

3.

4.

5.

Students find and circle the item that is different.
Categories are food and utensils.

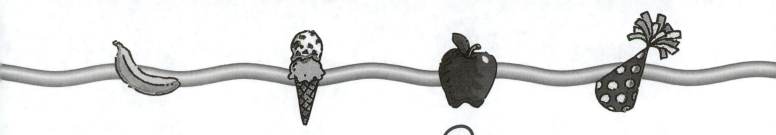

7. Listen. Color. Play Bingo.

Students listen and color. Then they listen and play Bingo, finding each item as it is named. They say, "Bingo!" if they cover three in a row.

 Listen. Circle.

1.

2.

3.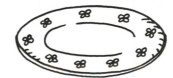

4.

5.

6.

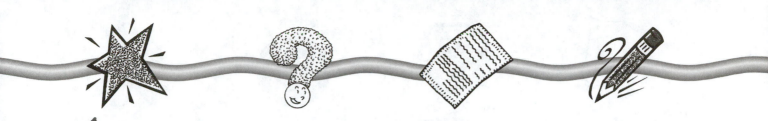

Units 7–9 Test

Listen. Circle.

1.

2.

3.

4. 9   10   7

5.

6.

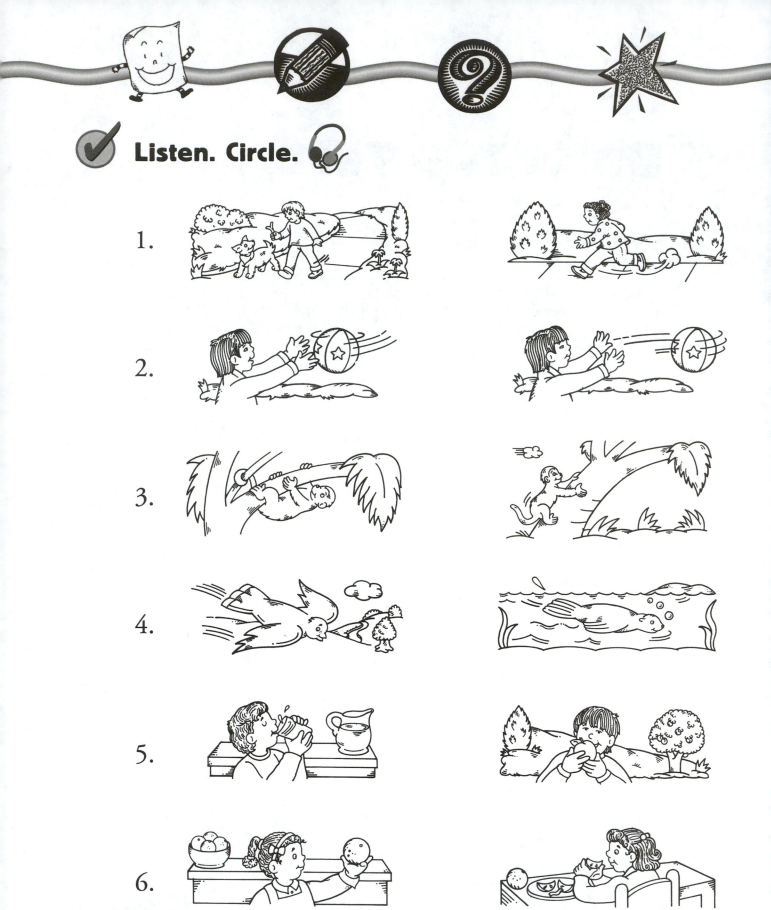

Listen. Circle.

1.

2.

3.

4.

5.

6.

Say what each circled person or animal is doing.

Language Activities Section

Contents

My Class

1. Draw.

How do you go to school?

2. Draw lines.

What is in the school?

Students draw how they get to school. They draw
lines from classroom objects to the school.

My Family

1. Draw your family.

2. Circle.

Find the people in the family.

Students draw their own families. They circle the family members from the story.

Move Your Body!

1. Draw a big smile.

2. Circle.

1. nose

2. fingers

3. toes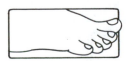

Students draw a big smile. They circle body
parts that the children move in the story.

Let's Play!

1. Draw.

What can you put on?

2. Circle.

What did the boys put on?

Students draw clothing. They circle the items the boys try on in the story.

My Toys

1. Draw a toy.

What is your favorite toy?

2. Look and say.

Find a toy. Point to it. Say the name.

Students draw a favorite toy. They look at a picture from
the story, then they point to a toy and say its name.

Lin Needs Help

1. Draw your house.

2. Circle.

Who helps Lin?

Students draw their homes. They circle the people who help Lin.

Come and Play!

1. Draw.

What do you play at the playground?

2. Circle.

What do they play?

1. climbing

2. hopping

3. running

Students draw their favorite playground activity. They circle
children who are climbing, hopping, and running.

Animals

1. Match.

Draw lines.

Monkey

Elephant

Seal

Lion

2. Draw one animal.

What is your favorite?

Students draw a line to match names of animals with their habitats. They draw a favorite animal in its habitat.

There's a Party!

1. Draw.

What do you eat at a party?

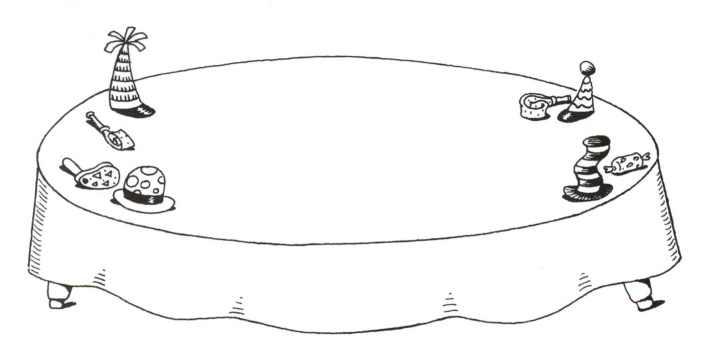

2. Circle.

Find the party food.

1. sandwiches

2. lemonade

3. cake

Students draw favorite party foods.
They circle party foods from the story.